soft pine whispers

t. kilgore splake

ISBN: 978-93-95224-39-0

First Edition: 2022
Rs. 200/-

Cyberwit.net
HIG 45 Kaushambi Kunj, Kalindipuram
Allahabad - 211011 (U.P.) India
http://www.cyberwit.net
Tel: +(91) 9415091004
E-mail: info@cyberwit.net

Printed in India at Quarterfold.

dedication

for william armitage jr

1945-2022

   this book is dedicated to my nephew, bill, whose life was an exciting and original adventure. he inherited from his smith family ancestors the definite 'carpe diem' attitude. during his existence, he indeed marched to a different drummer.

UNK

"no writing on the solitary, meditative dimensions of life can say anything that has not already been said better by the wind in the pine trees."

thomas merton

"few are altogether deaf to the preaching of pine trees. their sermons on the mountains go to our hearts."

john muir

"but high on mountains,
   the pines stand praying,
   their voices whisper low
   as they change together
   and ageless measure,
   reach out and up, and grow"

lorraine babbitt

"in snowbound, voiceless, mountain depths, to herald spring, pine trees sound in tune."

princess shikishi

# # # #

papa's ghost

big two-hearted shadows
holding fly rod and beer
nick adams rainbow dreams

# # # #

retirement bliss

nursing home day room
senior in rolling stone t-shirt
watching mtv reruns

# # # # #

creative nirvana

quiet coffee shop morning
only cook barista and writer
words rising in espresso steam

# # # #

illusions

free will to make decisions
forgetting ghost in shadows
virgin vagina virtue

# # # #

unknown darkness

death quietly closing
many other poets long gone
must think and write faster

# # # #

splake and gregory corso

one alone in wilderness
other standing on street corner
both possessing literary power

\# \# \# \#

fading green light

older woman flirting with poet
graybeard artist declining romance
unlike gatsby days of passion gone

\# \# \# \#

reflection

end of life's journey
poet asking
closer to mountain
or mountain now
something else

\# \# \# \#

simple as that

walking together
gently holding hands
soft wind blowing
her hair against my cheek
sunlight shifting through leaves
i turn to speak
like brautigan poem

\# \# \# \#

wilderness dream

naked young woman
swimming in brautigan creek
water dripping from breasts
running down thighs
making pussy wet
humming soft forest melody
full of river dreams

\# \# \# \#

dreaming of escape

forty going on forgotten
daughters no longer talking
mother with fuck me dreams
something romantic and exciting
like riding behind peter fonda
easy highway miles
tripping to new orleans

ain't fucking marching anymore

greatest generation graybeard
celebrating victory in europe
defeating fascism and hitler
also beating japan
now too old
to fight new american nazis
patriots wrapped in flag
like phil ochs song

\# \# \# \#

new sunday face

new church choir director
graduate of bible school
master's degree in musicology
husband home father
mother of nine children
grandson and granddaughter
enjoys singing and reading
also likes fucking

# # # #

missing out on life

high school star athlete
four sports letters
earning college scholarship
graduating with degree
business administration studies
becoming management executive
determined to increase profits
raise company's worth
leaving broken marriage
divorcing wife
estranged son and daughter
because being a winner
only thing that matters

# # # #

way life ends

f. scott fitzgerald wisdom
describing person's life
as process of breaking down
now running out of time
blind in one eye
slowly growing deaf
gnarled twisted toes
nails turning black
irregular heart rhythms
threatening fatal attack
living in achy sore body
crippling arthritic pain
no longer powerful
acting like strong man

# # # #

older poet dying
before quietly passing away
seeing elephants disappearing
to ivory hunter's guns
sacred giant sequoias
lost in fire ashes
lumbermen's chainsaws
oceans without whales
ahab's ghost in tears
for future artists
poets and painters
nature's solitary pleasure
alive wilderness evenings
watching young fawn
drinking from forest stream

# # # #

dream

young attractive barista
coffee shop mornings
cooking poet's espresso
only short while ago
playing with barbie dolls
having first period
small tender breasts
soft pussy fur
hiding quiet desires
asking graybeard poet
about lonely artist's life
like blond waitress
fellini's 'la dolce vita'
friendly voice saying
'save yourself
come with me'

# # # #

road trippin'

dark early morning
driving down empty streets
visiting local clinic
for blood chemistry test
quiet peaceful feeling
without truck radio noise
thinking lake michigan by dawn
noon passing over mackinac bridge
blowing quick few zzzz's
near chicago reststop
making breakfast menu
panaderia or outlaw kitchen
garbage restaurant omelet
with goat cheese and chilies
warm lone star beer
in wahoo old antone

# # # #

nature's heart

april ice out
spring waking from long sleep
forest wildflower blossoms
songbirds forest melodies
sharp pine tree scents
loud thunder and lightning
fierce summer storms
late autumn frost in air
colorful leaves falling
dry dusty haze
soon return of winter
season of long white
endless falling snow
while cold river waters
continue flowing on
carrying wilderness soul
into distant moon light

\# \# \# \#

agafon

for nephew bill

had serious dyslexic problems
understanding word meanings
trouble reading materials
mental health evaluation
measuring interpretive reality
doctor's final opinion
not schizophrenic but
determined driven poet
spending solitary years writing
literary biography stating
'it is not who i am
what i write matters'
soon forgotten obituary
with greek pseudonym
maybe bill's ghost with plato
both good and holy men

# # # #

rat bastard time

no more prom memories
'stardust' slow dancing
friday night gym sock hops
wildly shaking body
to rock and roll songs
passing on classical music
carmina burana and rites of spring
gershwin ravel stravinksy
npr's afternoon concerts
missing jazz evening blues
satchmo bird trane miles
lady day and ella
no longer climbing cliffs
hoping to meet
wilderness mountain lion
rogue forest black bear
missing trout season opener
angling rainbows and brookies
graying poet driven
to spend waking hours
continuously wrestling muse
writing about life
before time runs out

# # # #

free at last

memorized highway miles
between battle creek city limits
michigan's upper peninsula
crossing mackinac bridge
tripping into god's country
summer vacations
may to labor day freedom
mental health weekends
driving dusty backroads
cold six-pack at the ready
knowing below bridge exists
for tranny petrol fill
also roadside parks
necessary bathroom stops
now retired professor
escaping college campus
enjoying yooper solitude
quiet tranquil life
abandoning all connections
with lower peninsula flatlands
sad ignorant trolls
prisoners of rat race
without poetry in their souls

# # # #

shit happening

in autumn of poet's life
with death closing in
wondering in passing years
anything important happened
young boy growing up
going through school grades
getting college education
earning several degrees
traveling and meeting people
writing poems and stories
publishing several books
loving exciting sensuous women
untamed zelda fitzgerald beauties
caressing their lonely flesh
fathering sons and daughters
thankful healthy and successful
failing often with marriage
somehow unable to preserve love
surviving lonely hell of divorce
still looking for another woman
fruitless attempts at seduction
not wanting to die alone
in spite of life's bullshit
pissing time away

still staying on the path
enjoying life's exciting journey
not caring about the end

# # # #

c'est la vie

e-mail message
from old teaching colleague
professor of psychology
saying cognitively fine
but physically slower
selling his house
sante fe new mexico
moving closer to daughter
living in retirement center
sadly complaining
about years rapidly passing
seriously wondering
if i feel the same
curious about any solutions
really appreciate response
sad distant friend
not understanding reality
years eating and shitting
death being end
of human's existence
you fucking die
lives beginning
after leaving the womb
with slap on the ass

violent entry into world
mother's tender kiss
warm breast milk waiting
moment of birth
time clock begins ticking
young infant begins race
of what can be accomplished
before final breath
declaring last will and testament
after body's cremation
ashes to ashes
dust to dust
important to live now
'carpe diem' attitude
no fear of dying
having any regrets
knowing when time
to just let go
not passing away
in hospital or nursing home
warehoused with others
lost forgotten souls
dying awake in bed
slowly fading away
reflecting past life
successes and failures
after leaving earth
final remains deposited

in brautigan creek
flowing through cliffs
also granite monument
calvary cemetery
large black letters
reflecting i was here
peaceful wilderness place
where poet's ghost
wrestling with words
sacred holy activity
expressing beauty and truth

# # # #

9 789395 224390